CONTENTS

LOOK FOR THE REPTILE

Look for the *Dimetrodon* logo in boxes like this.
Here you will find extra facts, stories and other
items of interesting information.

LAND INVADERS

The story of reptiles started about 370 million years ago, when some fish managed to crawl out of the water and on to the land.

▲ Shallow waters teemed with life in the Devonian period.

Perhaps a drought, or long periods of dry weather, were reasons why fishes tried to leave the water. At this time, called the Devonian period, most of the world was very warm. Much of the land was covered by shallow lakes, which could have dried out from time to time. Fish in some of these lakes may have been stranded on mud flats when the water dried up. Some of them survived by using their strong fins to crawl to another pool or lake.

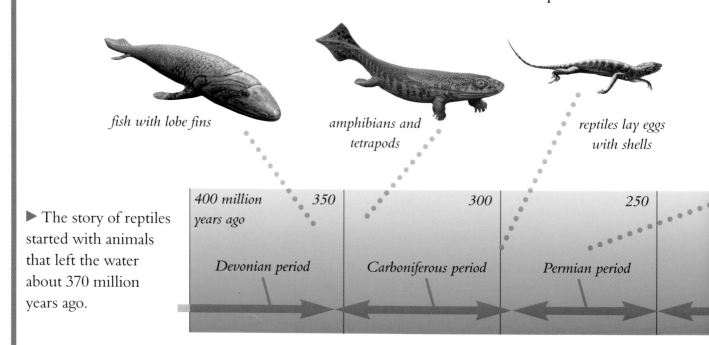

fish with lobe fins

amphibians and tetrapods

reptiles lay eggs with shells

▶ The story of reptiles started with animals that left the water about 370 million years ago.

400 million years ago	350		300		250	
Devonian period		*Carboniferous period*		*Permian period*		

PREHISTORIC ANIMALS

RISE OF THE REPTILES

MICHAEL JAY

Chrysalis Children's Books

First published in the UK in 2003 by
Chrysalis Children's Books
an imprint of Chrysalis Books Group Plc
The Chrysalis Building, Bramley Rd,
London W10 6SP

ISBN 1 84138 889 0

British Library Cataloguing in Publication Data
for this book is available from the British Library.

Printed in China
10 9 8 7 6 5 4 3 2 1

Acknowledgements
We wish to thank the following individuals
and organisations for their help and assistance
and for supplying material in their collections:
Alpha Archive: 4 (tl), 5 (t), 7 (bl, tr), 8 (tl),
   9 (r), 12 (tl), 13 (cr), 14 (bl), 18 (tl), 20 (tl),
   25 (br), 26 (tl), 28 (tl), 29 (br)
Corbis Images: 3, 28 (bl), 30
Gavin Page: 3, 7 (br),
Specs Art/Peter Geissler: 5 (bl), 14 (tl), 32
Specs Art/Steve Weston: 6
John Sibbick: all other illustrations

Editorial Manager: Joyce Bentley
Design and editorial production:
Alpha Communications
Educational advisor: Julie Stapleton
Text editor: Veronica Ross

▲ An evening scene
from more than 250
million years ago, as
three *Diictodon* reptiles
warm themselves in
the rays of the setting
Sun. Experts believe
that these animals
lived in burrows they
dug with strong tusks
and claws.

Descendants of these fish eventually started to breathe air and stopped living in water. They became the ancestors of reptiles, mammals and other land animals. But the changes did not happen overnight – they took million of years.

▲ All we know about ancient reptiles comes from fossils. the hardened remains of creatures, mostly shells, teeth and bones, that have been preserved in rock over millions of years.

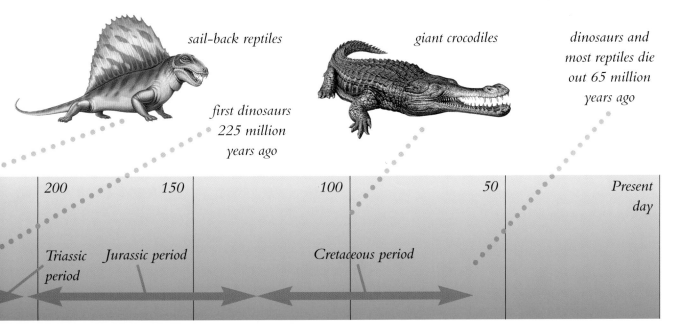

sail-back reptiles

giant crocodiles

dinosaurs and most reptiles die out 65 million years ago

first dinosaurs 225 million years ago

200	150	100	50	Present day
Triassic period	Jurassic period	Cretaceous period		

OUT OF THE WATER

The first animals to live partly on land were fish that had special fins. These fins, called 'lobe fins', had muscles and bones that gave them extra strength.

▲ *Panderichthys* grew about 1m long. It fed on smaller fish and other prey, possibly including insects.

One of the earliest lobe-fin animals was the *Panderichthys*, which lived in shallow ponds and lakes. In some ways it looked more like a land animal than a fish. It had no top fin and its four lower, lobe fins were rather like short legs. Perhaps *Panderichthys* heaved itself out of the water to snap at insects by the shore.

A LIVING LOBE-FIN

The coelacanth is a fish alive today that has lobe fins, the only kind to do so. It is 2m long and weighs up to about 80 kg. There are a few colonies of coelacanth living deep in the Indian Ocean. They do not use their fins to move on land though – instead the fins stir up mud on the seabed to find prey trying to hide there.

Over millions of years, some kinds of lobe-finned fish developed better ways of breathing air. In time, they became amphibians, animals that were able to live in water or on land. During this time, their fins became stronger and began to look like legs. Strength was important, because it is harder to walk on land than to float in water.

▼ Lobe fins had bones, so they did not need to change much to be suited for use on land.

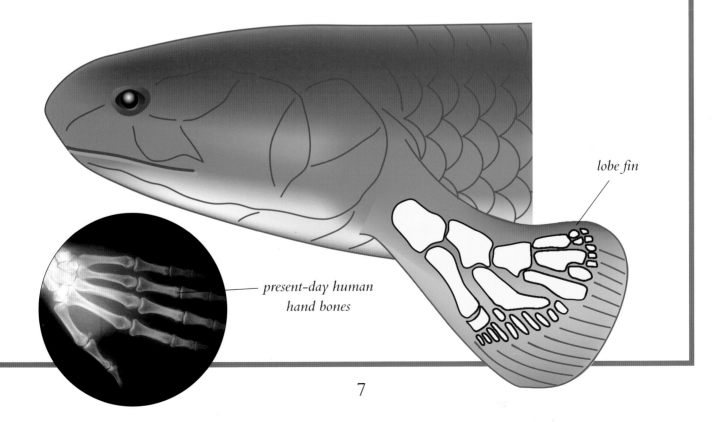

present-day human hand bones

lobe fin

THE TETRAPODS

Over millions of years, animals changed to adapt to new ways of living. Animals with backbones developed four limbs to move about. This became a standard pattern, which is called the tetrapod layout.

▲ *Acanthostega* had jaws lined with small but needle-sharp teeth. It ate mostly insects and small fish.

The amphibian *Acanthostega* and *Ichthyostega* are two of the earliest tetrapods known. They lived about 350 million years ago and grew 60 cm-1m long.

Acanthostega's four limbs had separate digits (like your fingers and toes) but each limb had eight digits instead of the five that later became usual.

Both these animals had limbs that were probably webbed, like a frog's, making them more useful as water paddles than for walking on land.

Most likely they lived in lakes and ponds. But they could move about on land, too, if there was food nearby.

▼ *Acanthostega* (in the water) and the slightly larger *Ichthyostega* chased small prey in the water and on land nearby.

A DESIGN FOR MANY ANIMALS TO COME

Animals with backbones (vertebrates) have the same basic body design. From rats to robins, hedgehogs to humans, they have four limbs, with separate digits.

Animals with no backbone (invertebrates) have body shapes and structures that are more varied, although all insects have six legs.

dinosaurs were tetrapods

birds are tetrapods, but their front limbs have developed into wings

insects have six legs, so are not tetrapods

humans are tetrapods

LAYING EGGS

Hylonomus *had scaly skin, much like a small reptile of today*

Amphibians like *Acanthostega* laid eggs in water. Reptiles were different – they laid their eggs on dry land. A tough shell protected the growing baby inside, until it was ready to hatch.

▲ *Hylonomus* grew about 20 cm long. It ate insects and other small creatures. Laying eggs on land was safer than leaving spawn in water, where most of them were eaten by other animals.

The earliest egg-laying reptile we know about is called *Hylonomus*. It was a small animal that lived in the warm Carboniferous period, about 300 million years ago.

Like today's turtles or snakes, *Hylonomus* laid its eggs on land, away from water. Strong, leathery shells stopped the eggs from drying out and protected the baby growing inside, which fed on the yolk.

We know about *Hylonomus* partly because of fossils that were found in Nova Scotia, Canada. Here there was once a forest where many trees died, leaving hollow stumps.

Lots of insects became trapped inside the hollow tree stumps. Bigger animals, including *Hylonomus*, jumped in after such easy prey – only to become trapped themselves and die of starvation. Eventually they turned into fossils, which scientists can now study.

▶ The *Hylonomus* hunted for insects and other small prey. Some *Hylonomus* chased prey into hollow tree stumps, where they could drown if there was water inside.

WATERPROOF COAT

Once they have hatched, amphibians need to stay near or in water to stop their moist skins from drying out. But reptiles developed a form of armour plating, so they could stay on land for long periods. This was a strong, horny layer that made a perfect waterproof coat. Many reptiles today, especially the big kinds such as crocodiles and alligators, are well known for their tough, thick skins.

STEAMY SWAMPS

▲ This Victorian-era drawing shows a coal miner standing next to a fossilised tree.

By 300 million years ago, the land was teeming with life, even though mammals and dinosaurs would not appear for about another 75 million years.

At this time, called the Carboniferous period, the Earth's climate was mostly warm and wet, and the landscape was quite different to that of today. Huge ferns grew out of lowland swamps, while giant trees more than 45m high towered overhead.

At ground level were animals that included millipedes 2m long. Huge cockroaches crawled over fallen trees, while buzzing overhead were insects such as *Meganeura*, a giant dragonfly.

Bigger animals in the swamps included the *Eogyrinus*, a 4m-long amphibian that was far larger than any early reptile. It lived much like a modern crocodile, staying in the water most of time. Every now and then it came on shore to snatch a land animal that strayed close to the water.

LAYING DOWN COAL

The Carboniferous period lasted from about 355 to 295 million years ago. It is often called the Coal Age, because most of the world's coal supplies were created then.

Over millions of years huge quantities of dead leaves and timber fell to the ground, the plant matter forming layers that were slowly squashed by the weight of material above, to be changed into a new form, which we call coal. Next time you see a lump, remember that coal is a piece of ancient forest that could be more than 300 million years old!

▼ Carboniferous swamps were vast, hot and steamy.

Meganeura *had a huge 70 cm wingspan*

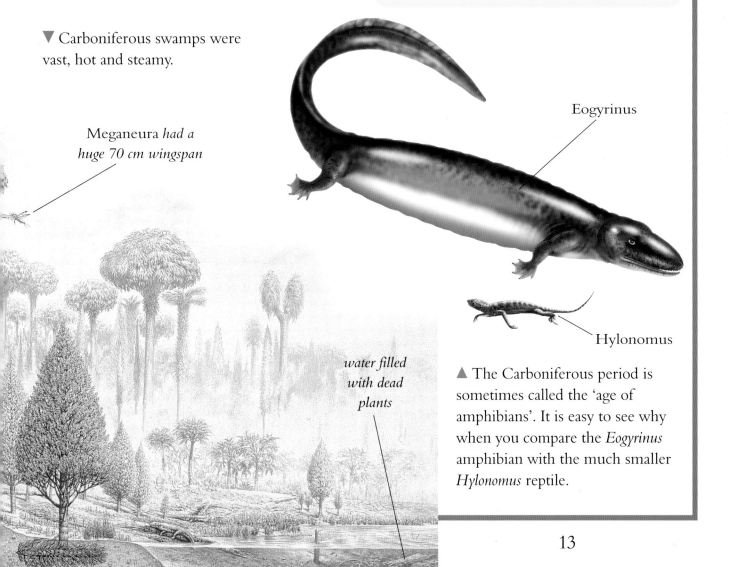

Eogyrinus

Hylonomus

water filled with dead plants

▲ The Carboniferous period is sometimes called the 'age of amphibians'. It is easy to see why when you compare the *Eogyrinus* amphibian with the much smaller *Hylonomus* reptile.

BOOMERANG HEAD

New kinds of reptile developed during and after the Carboniferous period. But many amphibians also lived then, including one with a head shaped like a boomerang.

horn on each side of head

flat body about 1m long

◄ *Diplocaulus* had eyes on the top of its head. It could lie safely on a muddy river bed, watching for prey passing overhead.

The strange-looking *Diplocaulus* lived about 280 million years ago. It was one of a group of animals with oddly-shaped heads. Scientists are puzzled by *Diplocaulus*'s head because there is no obvious reason for it to be shaped that way. The horns may have been used for fighting. They may have made *Diplocaulus* difficult to eat. They may even have been used as underwater steering fins when attacking prey.

PREHISTORIC CROAKS

The earliest known frogs lived about 250 million years ago. They were probably descended from creatures like the *Diplocaulus*. The early frogs looked similar to those alive today. They had no tail, no ribs and few bones in their backbone. They probably croaked mainly to attract a mate, just as modern frogs do.

► Also living at this time were amphibians such as *Cacops* (front) and *Casea* (middle). The fierce *Varanops* (top) was a 1.5m-long reptile with a mouth full of sharp teeth.

SAIL-BACK REPTILES

About 290 million years ago, there was a group of reptiles with large fan-like sails. The sail's skin was supported by spines growing from the backbone.

▲ *Dimetrodon* to scale with a human. It could run fast after prey, despite its bulk.

One of the fiercest kinds of sail-back was the *Dimetrodon*, which grew more than 3m long. An adult weighed about 450 kg – about the same as six adult humans.

Dimetrodon spent its days hunting other animals for food. It had wide jaws and teeth sharp enough to kill other big reptiles. The name *Dimetrodon* means 'two kinds of teeth'. It had large pointed teeth in front that could bite through flesh and muscle. Smaller back teeth were used to chew meat before swallowing.

◄ There were various kinds of sailback living at the same time as *Dimetrodon*. The ones shown here basking in the Sun were slow-moving plant-eaters called *Edaphosaurus*.

DRIFTING CONTINENTS

When *Dimetrodon* was alive, the continents were joined together in one giant land mass, called Pangaea. In this book we are talking about long periods of time and continents do move, even if it is only a few centimetres a year. Eventually the continents moved apart to reach the positions they have today.

the sail may have been brightly coloured for courtship displays

Dimetrodon's sail was probably used to control its body heat. Turning the sail to face the early morning Sun heated the blood flowing through the sail, helping *Dimetrodon* to warm up in a hour or so after a chilly night. Turning the sail away from the Sun or into a stiff breeeze helped *Dimetrodon* to cool off quickly on a hot day.

▲ Two *Dimetrodon* sailbacks bask on warm, sunny rocks.

SPIKES AND TUSKS

Some reptiles grew rows of strange, bony spikes on their heads. Others had huge teeth and tusks to help them eat tough plants.

The slow-moving reptile *Estemmenosuchus* was about the size of a modern cow and had lots of bony spikes growing out of its head. These looked dangerous, but the spikes were probably used for protection from other reptiles or used in displays when looking for a mate. *Estemmenosuchus* certainly looked fierce but most experts think it was a harmless plant-eater, because its teeth were better shaped for ripping off mouthfuls of leaves, not flesh.

▲ *Estemmenosuchus* lived from about 255 million years ago.

Another plant-eating reptile was the *Lystrosaurus*, which grew about the same size as a modern hippopotamus. It lived in coastal areas and had wide, spreading feet that supported it in soft, boggy places. *Lystrosaurus* probably spent most of its time rooting around in the undergrowth, looking for tasty plants to dig out with its pair of tusks or to snap off with its beak-like mouth.

BETTER BREATHING

An improvement in breathing allowed early reptiles to be more active than amphibians. Amphibians breathed (as they do now) mostly by taking in air through their moist skin, sometimes helped by using the mouth to fill small lungs. Reptiles used their ribcage as a big air pump, expanding the cage to suck in air and fill large lungs. The better breathing system allows reptiles to take in more oxygen at once. Because oxygen keeps the muscles working properly, reptiles can be more active than amphibians.

▶ *Lystrosaurus* may have lived in family groups, like hippos of today, hunting for food in the warm, muddy waters of streams and rivers.

DISASTER!

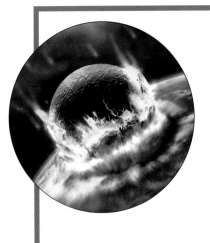

Most of Earth's land and water animals died out about 250 million years ago in a world-wide mass extinction at the end of the Permian period.

▲ Meteors are pieces of space rock. They range in size from tiny grains of dust or grit, to mountain-sized 'planet killers'.

There have been at least five great 'die-offs' or mass extinctions, in Earth's distant past. However, this was the biggest of them all, killing most life on Earth.

What caused this great die-off? No one is certain, but it seems that huge volcanic eruptions poisoned the air and seas for thousands of years. Red-hot lava gushed out of the ground, in a flood of molten rock that covered almost 4 million square km of ground. Some scientists also think that a huge meteor may have hit the Earth at about this time, making matters worse.

Whatever the exact causes, the effects were devastating – about 90 per cent of sea creatures and 70 per cent of land vertebrates died out. For most reptiles, life ended 250 million years ago. Only a few kinds survived in a world where most forms of life had been wiped out.

▶ Reptiles still fought each other even as volcanoes poured out clouds of ash and gas. *Anteosaurus* (left) was a meat-eater that preyed on other reptiles such as the plant-eating *Moschops* (right). Both these species died out about 250 million years ago.

DEATH FROM ABOVE OR BELOW?

Experts are divided as to why the great 'die-off' happened. Some studies have shown that a meteor punched out a 200-km crater in Australia, about 250 million years ago. This would have caused huge earthquakes and world-wide tidal waves. But other scientists think the disaster was much slower, with volcanoes pumping out gas and dust for about half-a-million years, during which many species became extinct. The final push was when methane gases bubbled up from under the oceans in a huge 'burp', causing global warming that was hot enough to kill off most remaining species.

THE SURVIVORS

New kinds of reptile took over after the Permian die-off, although life on Earth took millions of years to fully recover. New reptiles included the ancestors of dinosaurs, flying reptiles, crocodiles and mammals.

skin may have had hair instead of scales

▲ An adult *Thrinaxodon* is shown here with its pups. They were about the size of your hand.

Thrinaxodon was a 50 cm-long reptile that lived in the early Triassic period, about 245 million years ago. *Thrinaxodon* was part of a group called 'mammal-like reptiles' because they had similar teeth and bones to modern mammals and are thought to be the ancestors of mammals today. Fossils show that *Thrinaxodon* had sensitive whiskers, like cats and dogs. It also had big jaws and sharp teeth!

▲ *Euparkeria* had sharp teeth that curved back to keep hold of prey before swallowing.

Another group of reptiles, the archosaurs ('ruling reptiles') were the ancestors of crocodiles, dinosaurs and birds.

Euparkeria was an early archosaur that grew up to 60 cm long. It was a fierce meat-eater that walked on four legs most of the time. But it could run quickly on its long hind legs when needed. When running *Euparkeria*'s tail stuck out straight behind for balance.

 SLOWING DOWN IN THE COLD

Reptiles are cold-blooded. They keep warm by taking in energy from outside their bodies, mostly warmth from the Sun. At night or on cool days, a reptile's body temperature drops, and it slows down. Mammals are warm-blooded and keep a constant body temperature. They get energy by eating lots of food, and can stay active even when it is cold.

REPTILES AND MORE

Among the oddest reptiles were the rhynchosaurs. These plant-eaters were heavily built and for a time were common in many parts of the world.

Rhynchosaurs had long hooked beaks and strong jaws, with teeth that sliced through tough plants like giant pairs of scissors. In the middle part of the Triassic period, about 225 million years ago, rhynchosaurs were the commonest kind of plant-eating reptile. Also living at this time was a fierce hunting reptile, the *Saurosuchus*. This was a 7m-long monster that weighed more than a tonne.

By 225 million years ago, these reptiles had mostly died out. Their place began to be taken by early kinds of dinosaur, animals with long necks that browsed among plants and trees for tasty shoots and leaves.

◀ The *Saurosuchus* (top) was one of the world's fiercest reptiles about 220 million years ago. The plant-eating rhynchosaurs were very common at this time. The ones here were a kind called *Scaphonyx*.

Living alongside the reptiles were hairy little animals that darted about in the undergrowth, chasing prey such as insects and grubs. These were among the earliest mammals that we know about. It's easy to forget that mammals appeared about this time, because the age of dinosaurs would last for more than 140 million years.

It was not until the dinosaurs, along with most other reptiles, died out 65 million years ago that mammals had a chance to become important land animals.

▲ This giant-sized 'supercroc' lived about 100 million years ago.

NO PLACE TO HIDE

Tortoises, turtles and terrapins are the survivors of an ancient group of reptiles called the chelonians. Chelonians are different from other reptiles in an important way – their bodies are completely covered by a shell. The earliest chelonian we know about was a metre-long tortoise called *Proganochelys*. It lived about 220 million years ago and was quite similar to tortoises today except that it could not hide its head and limbs inside its shell.

▲ The early mammal *Morganucodon* was a small animal, growing just 13 cm long.

REPTILE WORDS

▲ *Acanthostega* was an early amphibian.

Here are some technical terms used in this book.

amphibian
An animal that can breathe in or out of water. Amphibians take in oxygen mostly through their moist skin and mouth.

archosaur
The 'ruling reptiles' that were the ancestors of dinosaurs.

chelonian
A reptile group that includes tortoises and turtles.

climate
A general word that describes the long-term weather patterns of a place or region.

coal
A hard black or browny-black material that can be burned as fuel. It is made from the remains of ancient plants.

cold-blooded
An animal, such as a reptile, that gets some energy from outside its body. After a cold night, it warms up in the Sun. Warm-blooded animals, such as mammals, get energy from their food, and do not need to slow down much in the cold.

dinosaur
A reptile group that lived from 225 to 65 million years ago.

extinction
When a group of animals or plants dies out completely.

fossil
The remains of a plant or animal preserved in rock.

global warming
A warming up of the Earth's climate. Can be caused by various things, including changes in the amount of heat given out by the Sun or by volcanoes erupting.

lobe fin
A kind of fleshy fin on some early fish. Unlike the fins of most fish today, lobe fins have muscles and bones.

lungs
The two spongy body organs used for breathing.

mammal
A warm-blooded animal that gives birth to live young and that feeds them on milk made in the mother's body.

meteor
A piece of space rock that hits the Earth. Most are tiny, some are many kilometres across.

methane
A colourless gas often used for fuel. It may have belched from under the oceans at the end of the Permian period, helping create a rise in global warming.

Pangaea
The name for the vast 'super-continent' formed when all the world's lands were joined up.

prey
An animal that is hunted by other animals for food. An animal that hunts others to eat is called a predator.

reptile
An animal, such as a crocodile, that is usually covered with scales or horny plates. Reptiles normally lay eggs, rather than giving birth to live young.

spawn
The soft eggs laid in water by amphibians, such as frogs.

tetrapod
An animal with four limbs that have separate digits.

vertebrate
An animal that has a backbone. Invertebrates, such as insects or jellyfish, have no backbone.

WEIRD WORDS

This pronunciation guide should help you say the names of prehistoric words.

Acanthostega
ak-an-thoss-teg-ah
amphibian
am-fib-ee-an
Anteosaurus
an-tay-oh-sore-rus
archosaur
ark-oh-sore
Cacops
cack-ops
Carboniferous
car-bun-iff-er-rus
Casea
kass-see-ar
Coelacanth
see-la-kanth
Diictodon
dy-ick-toe-don
Dimetrodon
dim-et-ro-don
Dinogorgon
die-no-gor-gon
Diplocaulus
dip-low-cor-lus
Edaphosaurus
ed-aff-oh-sore-russ
Eogyrinus
ee-gear-rin-us
Estemmenosuchus
ess-tem-en-oh-sook-us

Euparkeria
you-park-ear-ee-ah
Hylonomus
hill-on-om-us
Ichthyostega
ick-thee-os-tegga
Lystrosaurus
list-roh-sore-rus
Meganeura
meg-an-er-ra
Mesosaurus
mee-so-sore-rus
Morganucodon
more-gan-oo-coe-don
Moschops
moss-chops
Panderichthys
pan-der-ik-this
Pangaea
pan-geye-ah
Proganochelys
pro-gan-oh-chell-is
rhynchosaur
rink-oh-sore
Saurosuchus
saw-roh-sook-us
Scaphonyx
scaf-on-iks
Tanystropheus
tan-ist-roh-fee-us
Thrinaxodon
thrin-ax-oh-don
Varanops
var-an-ops

REPTILE FACTS

Here are some facts and stories about early life forms.

▲ The weird *Tanystropheus* lived about 220 million years ago. Its neck was twice as long as its body!

▼ Fossil of a reptile skull.

Fossil finds

Scientists learn about prehistoric reptiles by studying fossils, the hardened remains or imprints of living things preserved in rock over millions of years. However, only a few reptiles became fossils, as the bodies of most of them were either eaten by other animals or decomposed quickly after death. A typical fossil was made when a reptile sank into mud after dying. Layers of sand and silt built up over the top, protecting the remains until they were discovered millions of years later.

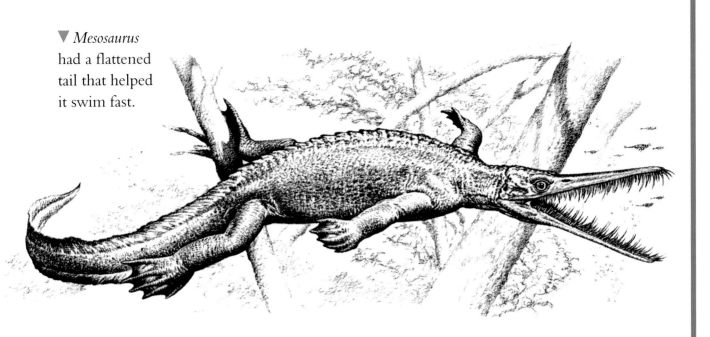

▼ *Mesosaurus* had a flattened tail that helped it swim fast.

Back to the water

Some reptiles left the land and went back to live in water. One of the first to do this was the metre-long *Mesosaurus,* which lived about 280 million years ago. It used a powerful tail and back legs to speed ahead, the front legs were used to steer.

Killer events

The mass extinction at the end of the Permian period killed about 90 per cent of life on Earth. However, there were at least two earlier extinctions, probably caused by climates changing quickly from ice ages to hotter times. There were also two later extinctions, the most recent taking place about 65 million years ago. It killed off the land-dwelling dinosaurs and most sea reptiles.

Reptile success

Reptiles are a highly successful group of vertebrates. Even though dinosaurs and their relatives died out, there are more kinds of reptile living today (over 6500) than there are mammals (about 4000). Most of the living reptiles are fairly small lizards, and even large ones like alligators and crocodiles are smaller than their prehistoric ancestors.

Wiggling walk

A reptile's legs stick out from either side of its body, so that when it walks its body twists from side to side. Most reptiles alive today walk like this. However, relatives of early reptiles, such as the dinosaurs, developed an upright leg position, which made moving easier and helped support bigger bodies.

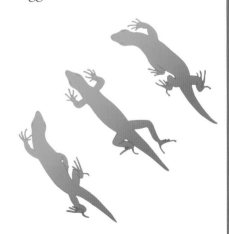

▲ A reptile twists its body as it walks.

REPTILES SUMMARY

The first reptiles developed from early four-limbed animals, sometime in the Carboniferous period, about 300 million years ago.

The first animals to move to land were fish with four strong lobe-fins. Later, amphibians could breathe both in water and on land. The four-limbed tetrapod layout became standard for all animals with backbones. The first true reptile was probably the *Hylonomus*, which lived in the Carboniferous period. It laid eggs away from the water, which were protected by having tough, leathery shells. Most forms of life were killed off in the Permian extinction of 250 million years ago. Reptile survivors included the ancestors of dinosaurs, alligators and turtles.

▼ The sabre-toothed *Dinogorgon* was one of many reptiles that died out at the end of the Permian peiod.

REPTILES ON THE WEB

You can find out about reptiles and other prehistoric animals on the Internet. Use a search engine and type in the name of a reptile or the prehistoric period you are interested in. Here are some good sites to start with:

▼ There are good sites that have information on prehistoric reptiles. Here are four screenshots.

http://www.sunshine.net/www/2100/sn2192/therapsid8a.htm

A detailed site with interesting facts on early reptiles. You can see many illustrations of the animals, drawn in a detailed style.

http://www.geocities.com/dinoman_pages/Dimetrodon.html

This page on the site shows a sail-back reptile, one of several early reptiles that are featured.

http://www.isgs.uiuc.edu/dinos/de_4/index.htm

This is a text-only reference site that has lots of information on many kinds of early reptiles.

http://www.bbc.co.uk/dinosaurs

This site features the TV series *Walking with Dinosaurs* plus material on earlier reptiles.

http://www.nationalgeographic.com/ngm/0009/feature4/index.html

This site has heaps of information on the great extinction at the end of the Permian period.

INDEX